Blackpool Trams & Recollections 1973 (Part 1)

Barry McLoughlin

Contents

Silver Link Publishing Ltd
The Trundle
Ringstead Road
Great Addington
Kettering
Northants NN14 4BW

Tel/Fax: 01536 330588

email: sales@nostalgiacollection.com
Website: www.nostalgiacollection.com

Acknowledgements

Many sources were used in the production of this book, but particularly valuable were Steve Palmer's series of erudite volumes on the Blackpool tramway; *Blackpool Tramways 1933-66* by Stephen Lockwood (Middleton Press); *The Blackpool Tramway* (The Tramway Museum Society); the ever-informative and sometimes trenchant *Trams Magazine;* and the websites of the Blackpool Heritage Trust: *www.blackpoolheritage.com/htrust/* and British Trams Online: *www.britishtramsonline.co.uk*.

But the most heartfelt thanks must go to the late Ray Ruffell, who had the foresight to take these wonderfully evocative pictures at a time when the future of the tramway was by no means secure.

All the images in this book are from the Ray Ruffell collection, which is held by the publisher. Ray was a railwayman, transport enthusiast and photographer of equal merit who travelled all over the country in pursuit of his hobby and his art.

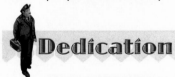

Dedication

To Billy and Max

First published in 2016

British Library Cataloguing in Publication Data
A catalogue record for this book is available from the British Library.

Printed and bound in the Czech Republic

Introduction

It was the best of times and the worst of times in 1973… with the latter dominating.

The Vietnam peace treaty was signed but otherwise the national and international news was almost universally bad, with inflation, industrial strife and IRA bombs in the UK, a global oil crisis, and war in the Middle East. Oh, and VAT was introduced The brighter news was more on the cultural side. After a period of stagnation – and whatever your views about them – new and colourful musical forms emerged, from Glam Rock to the release by Pink Floyd of their seminal album *The Dark Side of the Moon*.

Last of the Summer Wine began on TV, the first legal commercial radio station was launched and the first hand-held mobile phone call was made. But it was the economy that was to dominate the year in the UK, with the last day of 1973 seeing the launch of the infamous Three-Day Week. Prime Minister Edward Heath had announced the fuel-saving measure on 17 December after a year of industrial action by miners and other groups of workers, and a huge increase in oil prices by the Organisation of Petroleum Exporting Counties (OPEC).

Earlier in the year he unveiled a series of counter-inflationary policies, limiting wage and price rises, which sparked a wave of strikes by hundreds of thousands of workers.

Provisional IRA bombs continued to go off in Northern Ireland and Britain, though the signing of the Sunningdale Agreement was an early, but short-lived, step in the peace process.

The UK and Ireland joined the European Economic Community, as it was then known.

Abroad, apart from Vietnam, the news was nearly all bleak, with the Arab-Israeli Yom Kippur War, a military coup in Chile and the assassination of the Spanish Prime Minister.

We also lost some other heavyweight figures of the 20th century, including ex-US President Lyndon Johnson, Noel Coward, W. H. Auden, J. R. R. Tolkien, Pablo Picasso and Bruce Lee.

More happily, comic Peter Kay, athlete Paula Radcliffe and footballer Ryan Giggs came into the world, and Princess Anne married Captain Mark Phillips, though it was not to last.

In Blackpool, a fire devastated an amusement complex on Central Pier. Ex-England goalkeeper Gordon Banks switched on the Illuminations, Mike Yarwood, Freddie Starr and Danny La Rue were starring in summer shows, and the highly politically incorrect *Love Thy Neighbour* TV spin-off was at the Winter Gardens Theatre.

The pop charts were dominated by the likes of Sweet, Wizzard and Slade, whose perpetually played, pension-funding single *Merry Christmas Everybody* ironically sang out a tumultuous year.

Title page: **METROPOLE** III met at the Metropole… By 1973 Blackpool was the only town in the UK left with a traditional tramway, and competing with tramcars on the street-running sections was a new and sometimes disconcerting experience for many motorists. On 27 July, packed Boat tram 604 has been involved in a minor, slow-speed collision with an Austin 1100, on the right-hand side of the road which, unsurprisingly, has come off worse. Closer inspection reveals the car has apparently been slightly dented by a glancing blow. Meanwhile, twin-car 673/683 inches past on its way to Fleetwood. See page 27 for another picture of the aftermath of the collision.

STARR GATE The car park to the right of Coronation car 663, bound for Cleveleys on 28 July, is the site of the new tramway's ultra-modern depot at Starr Gate, which opened in 2012 with an eye-catching wave-effect roof. Beyond the car park are the chalets of the now-demolished Pontin's Holiday Centre.

STARR GATE Balloon double-decker 719 tilts into the camber of the tight curve on the turning circle at Starr Gate on its way to Little Bispham on 28 July. Across the crazy golf course is sister double-decker 710. Starr Gate formerly had links via Squires Gate Lane to the Lytham Road route, which closed in 1961, and, until 1937, to the separate tramway that ran through the sandhills to Lytham St Annes. The two cars parked in the foreground are on the left a Jaguar with the distinctive registration plate OJO 4F and next to it a variant of the BMC 1100/1300 range, KNF 510F.

PLEASURE BEACH The Pleasure Beach is the location of one of the two intermediate turning circles on the tramway: the other, less extensive, is at Little Bispham. On 28 July, the driver does a little DIY windscreen-cleaning on OMO car No 3, introduced the previous year. In the background are double-deckers 724 and 726.

Left: **PLEASURE BEACH** With its experimental tapered front ends, English Electric railcoach 618 approaches the Pleasure Beach turning circle on its way to Starr Gate on 28 July. Behind it is the famous Lucky Star amusement arcade, now Wetherspoons' Velvet Coaster pub-restaurant, which featured in the hit 2004 comedy musical-drama *Blackpool,* starring David Morrissey and David Tennant.

Right: **MANCHESTER SQUARE** On 3 August, Progress twin towing car 674 hauls its trailer, 684, past the Spa Hotel on the corner of the promenade and Rigby Road at Manchester Square. A fully laden landau heads in the opposite direction.

Left: **PLEASURE BEACH** A phalanx of Balloons on the Pleasure Beach turning circle on 30 July forms a 'tram sandwich' for solitary open Boat 603. The double-deckers are (from left) 708, 726, 710 and 720.

Right: **LYTHAM ROAD**
Apart from the fashions and the cars, this could almost be a scene from the golden age of street tramways, with a 1920s tram and Victorian boarding-houses. In fact, it's 3 August 1973, as engineering car 753, converted in 1958 from 1924-built Standard 143, heads from the depot along Lytham Road towards its duties on the promenade. Behind the tram, the track curves left into Hopton Road for the depot.

TOWER Next to the Tower building and the Woolworth's store, Coronation car 661 heads for Fleetwood on 22 July. The garish 1960s-style entrance to the Tower has now been removed to expose the original late-Victorian brickwork.

TOWER And this time the same car, Coronation 661, is at the almost identical location a week later, on 29 July, but heading south for the Starr Gate terminus.

Right: **TOWER** The spectacular honeycombed green façade of the Lewis's building was almost as much of a Blackpool landmark as the Tower until its demolition in 1993. Today the site is occupied by Poundland and also, until recently, by Harry Ramsden's fish and chip restaurant, which has since moved to the Tower building. Brush railcoach 630 passes on 24 July.

Left: **TOWER** At 2.05pm on 31 July, a pair of 1930s Balloon streamlined double-deckers, 700 and 703, waits at the Tower.

Left: **TOWER** Coronation car 662 has a full complement of passengers as it glides past the Tower en route to Starr Gate on 22 July.

Right: **TOWER** As shadows lengthen on 2 July, it appears to be standing room only on Brush railcoach 630 passing Lewis's department store on its way to the Pleasure Beach.

Right: **TOWER** Tram logjams like this were still a common sight in Blackpool in the 1970s. At the head of the queue outside Lewis's is double-decker 717, closely followed by railcoach 621, OMO car No 6 and Balloon 715. Wiser passengers might have chosen to hop on to one of Blackpool Transport's stylish cream-coloured double-decker buses, which were once as instantly recognisable as its trams.

Left: **TOWER** The one-man operated (OMO) cars were introduced from 1972 in an attempt to cut costs and increase income, but they were not particularly comfortable and therefore not hugely popular with passengers. Car No 2 works south past Lewis's and the Tower Lounge on 22 July.

TOWER Fares, please… a typically hirsute 1970s conductor collects fares from photographer Ray Ruffell's wife and daughter, Joan and Margaret, on board open Boat 600 at the Tower on 27 July. Not many creature comforts for the driver, with just a windscreen for protection…
The cars on the right include a Ford Anglia, an Austin Maxi and a Hillman Hunter.

NORTH PIER A fine line-up of streamlined trams at North Pier on 27 July. From the left they are Balloon 723 and railcoaches 625 and 637. The capped inspector on the right seems about to have a word with the driver of 637.

NORTH PIER Having left North Pier, Brush single-deck railcoach 632 passes Lewis's on 24 July heading for Starr Gate. It must be a hot summer as the driver has both his windows open. The banner spanning the road advertises Blackpool Zoo, which had opened the previous year. The former Burton's store is to the left of Lewis's, at the junction of Church Street.

1973
No 1 Records

January
Little Jimmy Osmond *Long-Haired Lover from Liverpool*
Sweet   *Blockbuster*

February
Slade   *Cum on Feel the Noize*

March
Donny Osmond   *The Twelfth of Never*

April
Gilbert O'Sullivan   *Get Down*
Dawn   *Tie a Yellow Ribbon Round the Old Oak Tree*

May
Wizzard   *See My Baby Jive*

June
Suzi Quatro   *Can the Can*
10cc   *Rubber Bullets*
Slade   *Skweeze Me Pleeze Me*

July
Peters and Lee   *Welcome Home*
Gary Glitter   *I'm the Leader of the Gang (I Am)*

August
Donny Osmond   *Young Love*

September
Wizzard   *Angel Fingers*
Simon Park Orchestra   *Eye Level*

October
David Cassidy   *Daydreamer/The Puppy Song*

November
Gary Glitter   *I Love You Love Me Love*

December
Slade   *Merry Christmas Everybody*

Above: **NORTH PIER** The Midland Bank in the background is now the appropriately named Counting House pub. On 28 July, one-man operated car No 7 waits at Talbot Square in the company of a very well turned out Austin Cambridge.

Opposite page top: **NORTH PIER** The 12 open Boat trams, officially known as 'improved' or 'luxury' Toastracks after the earlier generation of open tramcars, were the third member of the streamlined 'family' of cars introduced as part of General Manager Walter Luff's fleet modernisation in the mid-1930s. Entering service in 1934, they were built by English Electric and originally had an attractive green bow-wave on the livery at each end, adding to their maritime look. Unlike their exposed Toastrack predecessors, passengers' lower halves were protected by the enclosed bodywork to the waist. On 27 July, 603 waits for passengers for Gynn Square outside North Pier, followed by its siblings, a single-deck railcoach and a double-deck Balloon.

Below: **NORTH PIER** Blackpool's imposing War Memorial towers over the scene on the left behind Bispham-bound OMO car No 6 on 24 July. Travelling in the opposite direction, Balloons 705 (front), with the grand Clifton Hotel and the adjoining Clifton Arcade behind it, and 702 are followed by twin-car set 672/682.

NORTH PIER Freddie Starr is topping the bill in *Showtime '73* at the North Pier Theatre in this view on 22 July. Single-decker 679 was one of the former railcoaches adapted as twin-car towing vehicles but which could also operate singly without a trailer. In front of it is double-decker 718, which in 2016 returned to use as part of the 'B' fleet of modified Balloon trams. It was one of four Balloons that had been heavily rebuilt with flat ends, and later it received further adaptations including modified doors. In summer 2016 it re-emerged in wraith-like white after being secretly stripped of its previous advertising livery at Rigby Road.

NORTH PIER The Boats are perhaps Blackpool's most popular trams, at least on hot summer days. This is 603 at North Pier on 27 July. Several of these smart open single-deckers have been preserved as part of the Heritage Fleet, including pioneer 600, 227 (602) in fine red and white livery, and 230 (604) in 1970s green and cream. Four others are preserved in the USA while 236 (607) is at Crich Tramway Village.

NORTH PIER Perhaps the Boats' main rivals in the popularity stakes are the illuminated cars, such as the frigate *HMS Blackpool*, which is following OMO tram No 6 at Talbot Square on 25 July. *HMS Blackpool*, No 736, was converted from Pantograph car 170 in 1965. No qualms about cigarette advertising in those days…

NORTH PIER With a yellow and red colour scheme described variously as 'garish' or 'striking', new one-man operated car No 4 picks up passengers from the southbound shelter at Talbot Square on 24 July. The driver's ticket machine can be seen through the windscreen. Cars behind the tram include a Ford Escort and a Ford Anglia Estate.

Above: **NORTH PIER** 'Trams leave here for all stops to Gynn Square, Cabin Bispham, Norbreck and Little Bispham' reads the sign on the shelter at North Pier. On 22 July No 5 is going as far as Little Bispham. Close behind is railcoach 630.

Opposite page: **NORTH PIER** The elegance, breadth and concealed power – sometimes too much of it – of the Coronations are well captured in this view of 661 at North Pier on 22 July.

NORTH PIER Brush railcoach 625, built in 1937, has finished its journey to Talbot Square and will soon be returning south past a Boat car, three years its senior, on 27 July.

Metropole

METROPOLE Double-deck Balloon 718 coasts past the Metropole Hotel on the street-running section between Talbot Square and North Promenade on 25 July. Several schemes were put forward over the years to move the tracks to the seaward side of the hotel on Princess Parade to avoid tram/road traffic conflict, but none materialised. *The Day of the Jackal* is showing at the Princess Cinema. On the left, a pair of youngsters tries to beat the traffic.

METROPOLE Soon after the previous picture, Brush railcoach 621 heads south towards the Pleasure Beach. Immediately behind the tram is the Princess Cinema, now a Bier Keller. Doddino's Cafeteria and Masters Furnishers are long gone, the café replaced by a cabaret bar. Cars include two Jaguars, an Austin 1800, Sunbeam Alpine, a Hillman Estate, a Volvo, a Morris van., a Triumph Dolomite and several Fords.

Below: **METROPOLE** Crowds watch intently from the pavement as twin-car set 673/683 prepares to edge past Boat 604 en route to Fleetwood after the accident on 27 July shown on the title page. *Steptoe and Son Ride Again* is being screened at the Princess Cinema. The Boat tram, under its old number of 230, is now part of the Heritage Fleet and named *George Formby OBE*.

Above: **METROPOLE** In an example of the shared traffic system working properly, one-person operated car No 6 squeezes between the cars by Butlin's Metropole Hotel on 25 July. To the left of the tram a Mark III Cortina follows a Ford Anglia having safely passed No 6.

METROPOLE Illuminated car 736 *HMS Blackpool* sails past Butlin's Metropole Hotel in Princess Parade on a Circular Tour on 1 August. Cars include two Minis, an Austin 1100, a Triumph Herald convertible and a Ford Cortina Mark II.

METROPOLE A full Boat-load for 600 on 24 July as it passes Revill's Hotel to enter the street-running section to North Pier and the Tower… possibly an unsettling experience for the learner driver in the Ford Escort on the right.

Cocker Square

COCKER SQUARE Cocker Square was still an important, compulsory stop in the 1970s. Today, with the rationalisation of stops under the new LRT system, it no longer exists; the nearest stop now is Pleasant Street. In the next set of photographs, several open Boats are seen at Cocker Square. First, working a Coastal Tour on 1 August, is car 602, now part of the Heritage Fleet and running with its original number, 227. Another Boat is disappearing into the distance.

COCKER SQUARE The open Boat trams offer an exhilarating ride along the seafront. On 25 July, car 603 passes Revill's Hotel after leaving Cocker Square.

COCKER SQUARE On 1 August Boat 605 is poised to depart for the Tower. The conductor is collecting fares beneath the trolley tower…

COCKER SQUARE … and on 27 July Boat 606 – coincidentally with one of the wheel-mounted promenade sea-tour boats on the left – descends the slope towards Butlin's Metropole Hotel.

COCKER SQUARE On its way to Uncle Tom's Cabin on 31 July, 1953-built Coronation car 661 ascends the gentle climb north from Cocker Square. Sadly, the 56-seat tram, formerly numbered 325, has now been scrapped.

Right: **COCKER SQUARE** Brush railcoach 638 was converted into a one-man operated car, and painted all-over cream, in 1969, but the experiment was not a success and the front entrance was later removed. However, it retains its cream livery at Cocker Square on 1 August 1973 as it passes a Morris Marina and a Morris Oxford parked outside the Roscrea Hotel.

Left: **COCKER SQUARE** Queue at Cocker Square... Fleetwood-bound English Electric railcoach 615 (later OMO No 11) heads the line-up followed by OMO car No 7 and Balloon 719 on 31 July. The unadorned middle section of the listed 1863 North Pier stretches in the background on the right.

COCKER SQUARE Photographer Ray Ruffell's wife, Joan, and their daughter, Margaret, often joined him on his travels. On 29 July they are ready to board Coronation 663 at Cocker Square.

1973 Happenings (1)

January
The UK and the Republic of Ireland enter the European Economic Community
The Open University awards its first degrees
British shares fall £4 billion in one day
Aerosmith release their debut album

February
Rail workers and civil servants strike
US involvement in the Vietnam War ends with the signing of the Paris peace treaty
George Foreman defeats Joe Frazier to become world heavyweight boxing champion

March
Pink Floyd release *The Dark Side of the Moon*
Two IRA bombs in London kill one person and injure 250
Five days later bombs explode in Whitehall and at the Old Bailey
The Queen opens the new London Bridge
Seven men are killed in the Lofthouse Colliery disaster in West Yorkshire
Women are admitted to the London Stock Exchange for the first time
Bermuda governor Sir Richard Sharples is assassinated

COCKER SQUARE The high-rise Regent Court flats near Princess Parade provide some of the best views in Blackpool – the Tower, excepted, of course. On 24 July they form the backdrop as Balloon 723 heads south.

COCKER SQUARE The Progress twin-cars were introduced from 1958 as a way of dealing with the spike in passenger numbers during the summer season. Twin-car set 672 (leading) and 682 descends from Cocker Square on 25 July. The Renault 12 to the tram driver's left is parked rather closely to the car in front!

COCKER SQUARE One of the English Electric railcoaches that were rebuilt with flat ends similar to a twin-car, 611 became OMO tram No 12 in 1975 but was later scrapped. On the last day of July 1973, it makes its way along North Promenade near Cocker Square towards Fleetwood.

1973 Happenings (2)

April
Value Added Tax (VAT) comes into effect

British Leyland launches its new Austin Allegro range

Liverpool and Celtic are Football League champions in England and Scotland

The first call by hand-held mobile phone is made in New York

MPs vote against restoring capital punishment

May
1.6 million workers strike over pay restraint

The Ascent of Man, presented by Jacob Bronowski, is aired by the BBC

Sunderland beat Leeds United in a shock FA Cup Final result

Prime Minister Edward Heath speaks of the 'unacceptable face of capitalism' after the Lonrho scandal

Capital punishment in Northern Ireland is abolished

Princess Anne announces her engagement to Captain Mark Phillips

A Greek military coup abolishes the monarchy and declares a republic

June
A fatal house fire in Hull is later discovered to be the first of 26 fire deaths caused by arsonist Peter Dinsdale

Elections are held for the power-sharing Northern Ireland Assembly

Gynn Square to Cleveleys

GYNN SQUARE A predictably packed Boat 605 begins the short climb from Gynn Square to North Promenade on 1 August. It's billed as a 'Circular' tour though since the closure of the last of the resort's 'inland' routes a decade earlier, it's something of a misnomer, being more of an end-to-end trip. The Boats originally operated the Circular Tour via Talbot Square, the Promenade, Lytham Road and Marton, and resumed the tradition in 1957 when the tracks in Clifton Drive and Squires Gate Lane were uncovered. The much-missed Marton route closed in 1962.

GYNN SQUARE The old and the new at Gynn Square, North Shore, on 1 August. OMO car No 2 leaves for the Pleasure Beach while Balloon double-decker 711 picks up passengers on its longer trip to Starr Gate.

GYNN SQUARE In another view of Gynn Square on 1 August, English Electric Balloon 707 climbs on the next leg of its journey to Starr Gate while a sister double-decker stands alongside the shelter. Many of the Illuminations are already in place in preparation for the switch-on of the Lights in a month's time.

GYNN SQUARE The three-star Savoy in Gynn Square is one of Blackpool's grandest hotels. Brush single-deck railcoach 626 is about to pass it on 1 August.

Above: **BISPHAM** The conductor switches the trolley pole while the driver reverses the seats of Boat car 600 as it stands on the middle of the three tracks at Bispham Station ready for its journey back to the Pleasure Beach on 27 July. The prototype Boat, now sponsored by Fylde Tramway Society and named *Duchess of Cornwall* in 2007, entered service in January 1934, with lower side panels than the rest of the Boat fleet.

Right: **MINERS' HOME** The interiors of the open Boats are somewhat Spartan both for passengers and crew. On the front right, Ray Ruffell's wife, Joan, and daughter, Margaret, enjoy the ride as car 600 approaches the Miners' Convalescent Home on the way to Bispham on 27 July, shortly before the previous picture was taken. The home is now luxury flats.

1973 Arrivals

Crispian Mills	Musician (Kula Shaker)	18 January
Kate Thornton	TV presenter	7 February
Peter Andre	Singer	27 February
Jack Davenport	Actor	1 March
Chris Perry	Footballer	26 April
Noel Fielding	Comedian	21 May
Dermot O'Leary	TV presenter	24 May
Leigh Francis	Comedian	30 May
Jamie Redknapp	Footballer	25 June
Peter Kay	Comedian	2 July
Fran Healy	Singer (Travis)	23 July
Kate Beckinsale	Actor	26 July
Darren Campbell	Athlete	12 September
Ryan Giggs	Footballer	29 November
Monica Seles	Tennis player	2 December
Paula Radcliffe	Athlete	17 December
Paul Foot	Comedian	24 December
Matt Tebbutt	TV presenter and chef	24 December

This redrawn map is based on a rare pre-war sketch map and shows the Blackpool and Fylde Coast tramway network at its fullest extent, stretching almost 15 miles from Fleetwood to Lytham St Annes. The map is from the book *Great British Tramway Networks* by Wingate H. Bett and J. C. Gillham, published by the Light Railway Transport League in 1940. Although it is credited 'Supplement to Modern Tramway, June 1938', the line to St Annes had closed the year before, and the Layton and Central Drive routes in 1936. By 1973, all the 'inland' lines had gone and the tramway just ran along the coast from Fleetwood Ferry to Starr Gate.

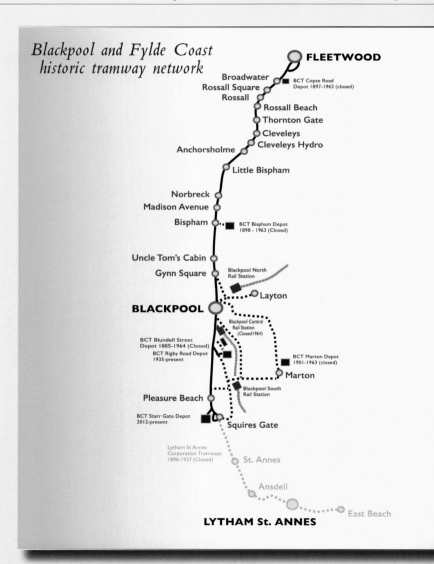

Blackpool and Fylde Coast historic tramway network

CLEVELEYS A congested scene in the centre of Cleveleys on 3 August: English Electric railcoach 615 (right) waits alongside its slightly younger Brush counterpart 634, which is behind Progress twin-car set 677/687. There used to be a roundabout at the square in the heart of Cleveleys but the complex junction of four roads and a tramway is now controlled by multi-phased traffic lights. Despite the fact that many trams reversed here, there was never more than a double-track layout, albeit with a crossover.

Index of Blackpool tram types

NORBRECK Photographed at Norbreck through the driving cab of twin towing car 680, Balloon double-decker 724 leads the way to the Pleasure Beach on 3 August.